Road to success

" How can I become successful ? "

By Balbacha El Mehdi

TABLE OF CONTENTS

I.   DON'T AVOID FAILURE

II.   DON'T BE NICE TO YOURSELF: GET OUT OF YOUR COMFORT ZONE

III. VISUALIZATION

IV. GET RID OF DISTRACTIONS

V.   BE MORE EXCITED ABOUT THE JOURNEY THAN THE PAY OUT

VI. SELF-CONFIDENCE

VII. MOTIVATION

VIII. YOU WANT TO AVOID BURNOUT

IX. HABITS OF SUCCESSFUL ENTREPRENEURS
1. They improve their daily habits
2. They WRITE down a strict schedule
3. They learn continuously
4. They focus on success: perseverance
5. They dream big
6. They keep a journal to track their progress

X.   LAST WORD: TAKE ACTION NOW!

ABSTRACT

What is success to you?

Some people understand success as a great accumulation of wealth. Others perceive it as helping others reach their full potential. It's for this reason that I took some time to write this book. I sincerely hope that it will help you push your limits and believe in yourself, so that you can finally live the life you dream of.

If you apply all the advices detailed in this little book, I assure you that you will be surprised to see the change it will bring about in your life. Indeed, I myself had, at one time, the mentality which established fictitious limits to my own potential. I suffered for a long time. I lived like in a bubble.

I was living in Poland at the time. Then, I returned to my native country which is Morocco to take the Baccalaureate there. For my university studies, I chose an American university in Morocco: Al Akhawayn University. From the first semesters, I took a few self-improvement and Critical Thinking courses. These considerably opened my mind.

As a result, I started reading books about self-improvement, and every night, I fell asleep while listening to speeches by world-renowned mentors: Gary Vee, Tony Robinns, Denzel Washington, Les Browns and so many others... When I woke up the next day, I used to play podcasts on YouTube while eating my breakfast. My days were dictated by these speeches that were so inspiring and motivating to me that I no longer recognized myself.

In reality, I have changed radically. I felt it, and I was so proud of it. At some points in life, you feel like you have learned everything, and that the learning process reached its end. However, it is precisely at this moment that we realize that there are so many other horizons to discover. Indeed, we all face several obstacles in our daily life. Some choose the easy path, which is giving up, while the others keep going. It is our ability to get rid of these obstacles that defines the intensity of our success.

This is why I invite you to read this short book very carefully. It will be of great help to you if you apply the methods detailed. You will, for sure, have moments of discouragement. But this writing learns you how not to give up! Really, follow these tips, and you will see the difference in a week, a month, or even a year. It is this continual evolution that will motivate you more to surpass yourself.

Let's not waste any more time, and let's get to the heart of the matter!

I. DON'T AVOID FAILURE

This may sound counter-intuitive as you're willing to succeed in your projects, but it is absolutely true and essential. Every successful person will agree with me on this point. Failure has to be seen as a blessing because it brings each one of us closer to his goals.

You need to perceive failure as lessons for the time when you will become successful. Keep in mind that, with time, you will become wealthier, happier, and you will acquire more responsibility. But several failures dot your path to success, and they will teach you how to live once you reach your goals.

These lessons include several aspects of life:

- ❖ **Time management**: how do you use the 24 hours that make up your day? Do you lose time on unproductive tasks? Could you do something faster by being more focused when doing it?

❖ **Social skills**: maybe you were an introverted person, but you noticed that it won't help you to reach your goals? Getting out of your comfort zone will be quite difficult at first, but believe me, it's the best thing to do.

❖ **Priorities**: what do you put first on your to-do-list? For instance, you will notice that overflowing your sleeping time by watching videos late at night might be a huge mistake. And this is only an example. You need to set priorities in order to reach your goals.

❖ **Self Confidence**: maybe you had an interview and you didn't succeed. Be happy! Now you know that there is no need to feel stressed out before going to such meetings (don't tell me that you didn't feel anxious!), and you also learned from your mistakes. Maybe there was a question you didn't prepare the answer for, or you didn't use sustained language. All these are some aspects that you will learn from for the future! Believe in yourself and in your capacities. You can do whatever you dream of!

❖ **And many others...**

Note: we will talk about soft-skills later on in this book.

So, every single time you face failure, you should feel happy. Every single person on Earth faces problems, but some have the ability of hiding it. This is the reason why you should never compare yourself to others, but rather see your failures as part of your personal growth. Don't think that you are a "loser" because you failed at something at which your peers succeeded. Believe me, they have certainly failed at much more aspects of their lives at which you succeeded, but the humankind is extremely talented at hiding their emotions / experience. And I know what I am talking about...

Some people face defeat without even growing. This happens when they remain lost, and they don't want to "wake up". Life isn't easy, but some people always try to find shortcuts. Yet, this gets them farther from their full potential than before. This kind of person want to stay in their comfort zone and live "peacefully". But what they ignore is that time will come when they won't find any emergency exit, and they will be forced to follow the path that life wants for them. And when life decides your living conditions, believe me that you will suffer! The reason is that they have never prepared themselves to growing up, and facing real challenges.

Yes, they grew up through time (which is natural), but their inner-self remained the same. This is extremely dangerous because, at some point, they will be forced to acquire some responsibility: founding a family, looking for a job, paying bills, help their children out and get them what they need and so on...

This type of persons has always lived with the fear:

- ❖ Fear of the future.
- ❖ Fear of the unknown.
- ❖ Fear of responsibility.
- ❖ Fear of missing the bus to work.
- ❖ Fear of being fired.
- ❖ Fear of not being able to pay bills.
- ❖ Fear of life in general.

And they will always remain in this state of mind until they choose to take control of their lives. The thing is that, when they will choose to follow the right pass, at that moment they have missed a lot of opportunities on the road to success. It will be harder, indeed, but it is still possible. What is better? Feeling worth respect by taking control of our lives, or always keeping the blindfold that makes us forget the reality in which we live? The first option is the best, right?

All this to say that you have to **take action as soon as possible**!

II. DON'T BE NICE TO YOURSELF: GET OUT OF YOUR COMFORT ZONE

It's simple. If you want to progress, you need to stop being nice to yourself. Why? Because action brings results, and most of the times, you will have to get out of your comfort zone to take the right actions. Namely, this zone will only bring you joy because you are used to taking the same actions. You know what will happen, and you don't experience (see / feel / say / do) anything new.

By being nice to yourself, you simply tell your inner self that he is doing a great job. Yet, if you want to reach your goals, you absolutely want to avoid this. To do so, you need to write down some things that seem challenging to you. It has to be written because the human mind isn't powerful enough to remember exactly what you set as goals. Said in other way, your brain doesn't really want you to challenge it with high expectancy, and will therefore make you forget about most of them.

This is why you absolutely need to write it down. It serves as a reminder, and as a comparison support to track your progress. It is a formidable weapon to get out of the comfort zone. Let's take an example to illustrate its importance.

Let's say that a random person, named Bryan, weighs about 105kg because of his bad diet. He doesn't want to go to the gym because his favorite activity is watching movies and eating junk food. Also, he says that he doesn't want anyone to see him in that shape, and therefore prefers to stay at home getting fatter and fatter, causing him to feel sadder, overwhelmed by the feeling of fear of any social interaction.

According to you, what should he do? Well, you would say that he needs to get to the gym, and not care about anyone's opinion because it is his life, and he is the only one to feel that bad, so he should take action for himself.

This is exactly the same for you concerning your current situation. Whether you want to get rich, improve your friendly or professional relationships, whether you want to lose weight to become a famous model or become a famous writer by publishing books, it is imperative that you get out of your comfort zone and that you take action now! Being nice to yourself won't get you anywhere, on the contrary.

As stated by the American economic magazine *Forbes*, successful people "are constantly learning new things and have new experiences. They aren't afraid to try new activities and to fail at them". So, what are you waiting for? Set goals for a defined period, preferably on a daily basis, and for the end of the month, and get out of your comfort zone!

III. VISUALIZATION

This is an incredibly effective faculty that you can use to make dreams become real. Visualization increases the likelihood of your goals and dreams. Jack Nicklaus, one of the greatest golfers in the world, once said (*unfinishedsucces.com*):

"I never hit a shot, not even in practice, without having a very sharp in-focus picture of it in my head. It's like a color movie. First I "see" where I want it to finish, nice and white and sitting high on the bright green grass. Then the scene quickly changes, and I "see" the ball going there: its path, trajectory, and shape, even its behavior on landing. Then there's a sort of fade out, and the next scene shows me making the kind of swing that will turn the previous images into reality"

<u>Jack Nicklaus</u>

Moreover, a study was conducted by Dr. Biasiotto (University of Chicago), which showed how important the role of visualization is in reaching goals. To do this, he split people into three groups:

1. Group 1: Practice free throws every single day during 1 hour (30 days).
2. Group 2: Visualized themselves making free throws every day (30 days).
3. Group 3: Practiced & visualized themselves making free throws every day (30 days).

Then, at the end of this 30 days' period, he recorded the improvement of each group. Here were the results:

The first group improved its results by 7% while the second improved by 10% (without doing a single throw, but by visualizing the scene). On the other hand, the group of people that practiced and visualized themselves making free throws improved its results by 32%!

But how is it possible?

Well, our brain is an extremely powerful machine that needs to be used wisely. If not, it can constitute a formidable enemy against our personal development.

Our brain is composed of neurons, thanks to which signals and action potentials are transmitted at the level of synapses: chemical and electrical synapses. The human brain is constituted of 100 billion neurons. These don't reproduce / regenerate.

They interpret images as real life. The images they receive either come from what our eyes perceive, our what we have decided to create in our mind. As a consequence, our body receives orders to act as if those images were real. For instance, if you envision yourself swimming, your neurons receive an impulse that tells them to perform such a movement. Consequently, our body will do so.

Do you understand now? The more you will visualize yourself at the stage you want to reach, the more likely it will happen because your body will act as such. This is much more powerful than you can think. Give it a try.

Here are some tips that will help you do it effectively.

❖   First, you need to focus on small details. It's extremely important because your brain, and therefore your body also, will perceive it as real. For instance, if your goal is to become the next best basketball player ever, you need to imagine yourself scoring amazing free throws, two-point shot, three-point shot or dunks. You need to hear it; you need to feel it. You can feel your calves contract during the jump, the ball leaving your hand, and your feet getting back to the floor. Then imagine the ball flying before crossing the basket net and falling on the floor. You may imagine the team you will be playing with, the championship that you will be fighting for, the number of people sitting there and watching you scoring amazing goals.

❖   You really need to visualize it by limiting any type of distraction. Do it as often as possible, and every time, you will feel closer and closer to your goal. To exercise this faculty, and develop it, you can train by looking at several objects / colors in front of you. Then, you want to close your eyes and picture what you have just seen as precisely as possible.

This is an extremely important point that you need to focus on.

Now, I want to get to the fourth point, which I have mentioned right now. But this time, I want to talk about it more in depth.

IV. GET RID OF DISTRACTIONS

It's easy to divert our focus to something that seems easy, and that we may be used to do. It can be watching TV instead of training, listening to meaningless radio channels than audiobooks, or going to the club during the week-end rather than developing your business. Of course, you need to enjoy this journey during which you work in order to get to where you want to be (we will talk about it in the next point). But what I mean is that you need to get rid of such unproductive moments, as much as possible.

To do this, you may want to write a list of time-wasters and keep yourself accountable not to do them. It has to be a list that suits your lifestyle. You may want to keep going to the club every week-end because you know that the next day you would be extremely productive, and this is what you want! It's important to be honest with yourself, and check what you need to get rid of. Focus on what is the most important for yourself.

It's also extremely essential to keep activities to let your brain rest:

- ❖ One to keep in shape: gym, basketball, running...
- ❖ One to build your knowledge: read a book.
- ❖ One to develop your creativity: draw.
- ❖ One to learn soft skills: go out, and interact with strangers.

Now that you understood that avoiding failure won't get you closer to your goals, that you should do your best to get out of the comfort zone, that you realized how important visualizing is, and that you wrote a check-list to get rid of distractions, I want to get to a very important point: appreciate the journey, and make it fun.

V. BE MORE EXCITED ABOUT THE JOURNEY THAN THE PAY OUT

Remember that we will all die a day. Life is a game that you witness through your eyes, and you act depending on the orders given by your brain to your body. You don't know how much time you will remain in this game, so don't let your emotions take over. I agree with you, when you visualize yourself at some point that you dream of since a long time, all you want is to be there as quickly as possible.

Yet, what I want you to understand is that, by enjoying the journey, you will be more efficient. Indeed, you won't be as affected by a failure than if you were only thinking of the end of the road to success. Once you will reach that goal, being a basketball champion at a worldwide scale for instance, you will want more.

Your life shouldn't be relying on the satisfaction of being at that point, but you should rather enjoy the journey as well as the final reward.

Hard work pays off. Successful people <u>don't want</u> to become rich with "rich quick schemes", but they rather focus on "building sustainable careers through hard work, risk taking and creativity" (*Forbes*). Despite all the obstacles that you face, you need to keep going and enjoying the fact that you are doing the right things the right way (hard work).

This way, you will enjoy even more the reward. Look at it as a game (because it is a game), and try not to make it too serious. You will start feeling yourself carrying a lower emotional weight, gaining perspective and finding new opportunities.

Now, let's talk about self-confidence.

VI. SELF-CONFIDENCE

Well, you may have read so many articles, books, and magazines talking about the importance of self-confidence. Well, I say it again, it's necessary, if not the most influential factor, that will lead you to success.

First because having a lack of confidence will lead a person to inaction. We talked about it in the "comfort zone" part of the book with the example of a random person named Bryan, who is scared of going to the gym because of his shape. He is scared of people's opinion because he believes that he is not "worth admiration".

Instead of looking for solutions to remedy this unpleasant situation, Bryan prefers to stay at home, so that no one can see him. That seems counter-intuitive because if he wants to lose weight, he has to get to the gym, right? The more he stays home, the fatter he will get, right?

Note: we are not talking about home-workout / changing diet simply because it requires even more motivation, and we will talk about this point later on.

This means that a lack of confidence always leads to inaction, and not standing up for what is really important for oneself. This way, people set the bar too low, and therefore they don't have much energy to reach their goals. It's because Bryan isn't confident about his shape, and what people will say about him, that he chose not to go to the gym.

On the opposite, <u>confident people start things</u>: they are **doers**. They strike out on new ideas even if people around them remain pondering it. They believe in their beliefs, and therefore in their actions too. Whenever they begin a new project, they do it until the end, not matter what the others may think / say about it.

Also, confident persons stand up for themselves. This means that whenever they talk, people listen to them. Just look at public figures, for instance the former American President Barack Obama.

Studies rated President Obama as having the highest self-esteem of all the candidates in 2008. It's because he believed in his own ideas that he was able to run for two terms before leaving the political scene. In addition to the fact that he ruled the most powerful country in the world, he attracted the trust of many of the foreign politicians with whom he worked closely thanks to his self-confidence.

The President crowned Nobel Peace Prize in 2009 could stand up for his beliefs, even for major decisions: agreements with Iran and Cuba, Climate Change treaty (Agreement of Paris in 2015), Obamacare…

You must be inspired by the major figures on the world stage. They are the perfect example because once, they were lost, just as you are now. They lacked self-confidence and motivation. At a time, they didn't use visualization as a tool to reach success. But one day, they simply decided that they could make it up. And they did it!

Take the example of:

❖ Warren Buffett, who was a newspaper delivery boy. Actual net worth: $77.6 Billion.
❖ Oprah Winfrey, who was a grocery store clerk. Actual net worth: $2.6 Billion.
❖ Jeff Bezos, who was grill operator at McDonald's. Actual net worth: $110 Billion.
❖ Michael Bloomberg, who was a parking lot attendant. Actual net worth: $55.5 Billion.

Note: Net Worth data was found on *Investopedia.com*.

What you should learn from this is that, whatever your current situation looks like (professionally or financially speaking, your relationships with your friends / family, or your grades in college, your physical shape, your skin color...), you can make it. All you need in order to achieve it is self-confidence.

Being self-confident helps you say **no** to whatever seems to distract you from your goals, and **yes** to opportunities, whatever other people's choice is. You don't have to do something that people agree with, otherwise your results will look just like theirs.

It will also push you set the bar high enough to challenge yourself, and see a huge difference between the person you currently are, and the one you will be in a period of time (one month, half a year, a year, a decade...). It will be a **day-to-day** self-improvement.

With self-confidence, you will stretch your limits. If you can run at a pace of 5.5 mph at the gym, the next day you should run at 6.0 mph and so on... If today you can read a book at a pace of 20 pages per hour, tomorrow you should read 25 pages! The simple reason behind this is that, from now on, you believe in yourself. You believe in your capacities, and you know that you can do it! Nothing can stop you anymore, you are finally at the control of your own life. Believe in the process, and stay focused.

This said, it's time to talk about motivation.

VII. MOTIVATION

We usually say that motivated people are "driven". Yes, they are <u>driven by their goals</u>. But for what reason are they so motivated to succeed in their life? Well, they attach feelings to these goals. It can be the result of something they lived during their teenage years (poverty, violence…), or the feeling of being underestimated by society.

They are <u>driven by real reasons</u>. In fact, some people believe that they are motivated just because they say that they want to do something. Yet, this is not the way they will remain motivated in the long-term. Remember, to achieve something that is huge for oneself, you really need to feel something inside of you that tells you that it's the right thing to do, that you "have to do it".

Don't wait for the "right moment" to do it because there is no "right moment" to begin. Every single second is the right moment to begin. Whenever a lion sees a prey in the jungle, it doesn't wait, but it takes action. Yes, you are going to tell me that it is the survival instinct that drives that lion not to think before taking action. And that's the point!

You really need to act as if your life is at stake, and that you don't have the choice, except following your dreams. This is the way you will be "driven".

You should also hang out with positive people that motivate you. Yes, the entourage is extremely important because it influences your state of mind. A famous saying states:

"Show me your friends, and I'll show you your future"

Your friends play an extremely important role in your success. If you hang out with losers, you are likely to become a loser. If you hang out with winners, you are likely to become a winner. That's some kind of mathematical equation where your friends act as the X variable, which results in your future (Y variable). As simple as that.

Surround yourself with motivating people! The reason is that you will meet them almost on a daily basis, and you won't want to be inferior to them and they won't as well. As a result, it will be a friendly race leading each of you to surpass yourselves. They will have an extremely positive impact on you.

Consequently, you will learn how to speak "their language": the well-driven one that every successful person speaks.

Communication skills are the key to understanding every single person your will interact with throughout your life. By being a positive speaker, you will attract positive ones. See the glass half full, and not half empty. Whenever you want to say something, try to not be rude, or impolite. This way, you will motivate those around you, and they will consequently also do so. Act as a magnet of positive energies.

Be positive to others, but also to yourself. Whenever you want to give up, or when you feel lost, just affirm to your inner self the following statements: "I'm good enough to do it"; "I set this goal, and I will achieve it"; "I want to learn and succeed"; "I'm strong enough to do it"; "I'm close to my goal". The most important thing is that you never give up.

Find whatever motivates you, and put it in the center of your life. Whether it's money, helping others, feeling that you did something great to yourself or your family at the end of the day, you have to put it in the center of your attention. This way, you will reduce the chances of getting out of the way to success. All you need is motivation and focus.

But it's important to give yourself some rest because what you absolutely want to avoid is burnout.

VIII. YOU WANT TO AVOID BURNOUT

Yes, this is so essential!

This is part of stress management, but also time management. You see? We are always talking about soft skills to achieve your goals. I can't say it enough, but it's so important to develop your soft skills! You love what you are doing, you feel that you prefer staying up working rather than loosing 6 or 8 hours sleeping. You feel so motivated that nothing can stop you!

Congratulations! This is an amazing gift! But what you absolutely don't want to fall into, is burnout. Try to find harmony between all your activities. Pablo Palatnik, founder of the sunglasses shop *ShadesDaddy*, once said:

> *"I think most entrepreneurs will tell you it's impossible to unplug – so burnout is almost inevitable. However, it's important to know when you're close to or at a burnout stage. Something as simple as taking a day off, going for a bike ride, or having a fun night out with friends can help to take the edge off."*

Pablo Palatnik

Do you understand? You need to enjoy what you're doing, but try to find your breaking point. Use as much energy as you can, that's very important, if not essential to success. But it's as important as taking a break at the right moment. You can schedule it on a daily basis in order to maintain the same schedule in the long term, and be more performant.

You will gain in productivity by scheduling some free time every single day, and sticking to it. You shouldn't think that it's smart to go for 15 straight hours. This would eventually have the opposite effect. You absolutely need to schedule free time, as mentioned by Evrim Oralkan (founder and CEO of Travertine Mart):

"Schedule free time on your calendar, just like you would schedule a meeting, and stick to it. It's crucial to take the time you need for yourself, even if it's just 30 minutes a day. You'll get back to work feeling recharged and inspired, and chances are, you'll accomplish a lot more than you would if you worked straight through the day."

Evrim Oralkan

Avoiding burnout also includes working out. You simply unplug from everything related to business, and you can focus on yourself. It can be fitness, a long run or a four-hour bike ride around the city. Once you will be done, you will have the opportunity to make a fresh start as you will lose all stress you may have generated at work. New ideas may come to your mind.

IX. HABITS OF SUCCESSFUL ENTREPRENEURS

If there are two things that set successful entrepreneurs apart from ordinary people, it is their strong mindset and their determination and dedication to daily success. Whether we talk about Elon Musk, Steve Jobs or Mark Zuckerberg, all are having successful entrepreneurial careers. How? 5 main steps led them to this success, and we will have an overview of them in the following paragraphs.

1. They improve their daily habits

It is true that being independent from everyone on a daily basis is THE strong point of entrepreneurship, or at least one of the strong points. But be aware that it is a double-edged sword.

Indeed, if you know how to manage yourself to being autonomous on a daily basis, then it will be beneficial for you. But if you don't get rid of bad habits, then you will be the only person to be affected. Not your friends, nor your family. Only you.

Can't you really see what I want to come up to? Fine, here is an example:

If you go to Starbucks every morning to drink a Cappuccino because it has become a habit (even an addiction), then it will be necessary to sacrifice this moment of unproductive pleasure for a more productive activity. Yet, you can go there and read a newspaper to learn about entrepreneurial news, or you can take the opportunity to write your planning for the day (you can even find out an opportunity that you can seize during your day thanks to this productive moment you have spent while drinking your

Starbucks Coffee).

The second extremely important point I want to talk to you about, is writing down a schedule.

2. They WRITE down a strict schedule

You will tell me "but why should I write a schedule if I know what I will be doing during my day? I have everything in mind, just as everyone, don't worry". And that's the point. You don't want to do like everyone else because you are aiming to reach much more than the others. It's time to reach your full potential! Leave your past behind and forget about it. Now that you bought this book, it's time to change, and become the best version of yourself.

So, write down a strict schedule!

By having a written schedule, you will be able to include more ideas that will push you forward. Let me explain myself.

If we refer to Elon Musk, the latter dedicates Monday and Tuesday to his SpaceX business, Wednesday and Thursday to Tesla, before combining both on Friday. You have to think the same way as successful entrepreneurs if you want to reach the top in your entrepreneurial career.

If you create an ideal schedule the previous day, but that the next day you only respect 60% of it (which will certainly happen), you will be able to reach 70% of it the next day, and so on. Once you've successfully completed this schedule, and that you feel that you became comfortable with it, then it's time to add a challenge. The goal is to optimize the use of the 24 hours that make up every human being's day.

We all have 24 hours in our day, without exception. Some of us spend those hours on leisure and instant pleasures, while others spend their time on activities that bring them closer to their goals. Let's take the example of audiobooks.

If you used to spend 1 hour of your day on the road listening to the radio, and then 30 minutes reading a personal development book, then it would be wiser to save 30 minutes by dedicating the whole hour in the car listening to audio books. The advantage is threefold: in addition to saving 30 minutes of reading, you will benefit from a full hour of learning (twice as what you used to do), and you will feel a sense of full satisfaction as you are on the right path.

You can use those next 30 minutes calling a friend of yours, watching a video, or reading newspapers! What you need to let your inner body understand is that that one hour spent on the road isn't a loss, on the contrary. Once you feel that it became a habit, you can "raise the difficulty level" by spending the next 30 minutes reading self-improvement books, and so on...

The success of each person is in book-reading. Without even noticing it, you have already saved 1 hour of your day, and you have invested it in a meaningful activity. Your best investment is yourself!

3. They learn continuously

You can ask any successful person around you. If there is one thing they will mention as being mandatory in their success, it is NON-STOP learning. I repeat: your best investment is yourself!

Even the brightest entrepreneurs recommend daily books reading. Whether it is Bill Gates, who reads 50 books a year, or Warren Buffet, who spends 80% of his days reading, everyone invests time on a daily basis for learning.

Human brain is the best machine that has ever been designed, and it is fed by being constantly stimulated. New ideas and concepts have to come across this amazing organ in order to keep it healthy and operational. You don't want to put it aside because that would cause its deterioration through time.

You can read articles exposing news concerning your professional field. It can talk about entrepreneurship, and new opportunities in the city / country where you are currently working, new taxation rules that apply to your firm (you can see yourself saving much more by staying up-to-date for such important data), or new ways of maintaining good quality raw materials if you work in such industries.

Suppose you are the founder of a cement delivery start-up. In short, you are the intermediary between the supplier and his customer. In this case, it would be interesting to read books on "development of start-ups", "customer loyalty" in order to broaden your knowledge in this domain, helping you improve your products' delivery in the future for instance. Or, you can read newspaper articles dealing with the cement market, the most promising fields, announcements (recruitment, low-cost sales, etc.) ...

You may also choose to read self-improvement books.

There are some books which have proven to be very useful for everyone, especially for people wishing to change their lives by learning soft skills. We may think about R. Kiyosaki's *"Rich Dad, Poor Dad"*, *"How to Win Friends & Influence People"* (Dale Carnegie), or Napoleon Hill's *"Think and Grow Rich"*. This said, you shouldn't lose time, and you have to learn soft skills.

Degrees aren't as important as soft skills because the latter are those that will accompany you through your days:

❖ Are you persistent when you have a goal in mind?
❖ Do you give up when facing the first obstacle?
❖ How about your social skills? Are you an introverted person?
❖ Are you able to give up on your bad habits when it becomes mandatory in order to reach your full potential?

All these are questions that you should ask yourself. Whenever you feel hesitating before answering any of these queries, you have to focus on that particular point. By reading several books, you will question yourself even more. This will help you get closer to what we refer to as "the best version of ourselves".

What you need to understand is that you can never reach that point, which is in fact even more motivating. By nature, the humankind has to remain imperfect. But those imperfections are so well-hidden that some of us prefer not to solve them, but they rather choose to remain in their comfort zone. This sadly applies to most of us.

But you bought this book to see real change in yourself as a person. This is why you have to set yourself apart, and look at these aspects.

What you also need to understand is that you will never have a large-enough knowledge about any area in life, even the one that you have most knowledge about. In fact, there are always some things that are missing. The human mind is conceived to learn new things, and forget about others. This is why you always need to fill it with new data because that will train it to become more performant.

Over the course of the days, your priorities will change and the themes of your readings will also change. As a consequence, your knowledge will expand to a greater number of areas. You will, for sure, get the pay-raise that you are asking your employer for since months (if not years) if you have great knowledge. Who can resign to an employee who can adapt to all types of business partners? Very reassuring for the latter, this kind of person can follow any conversation and thus streamline negotiations for instance.

Indeed, if you manage to enlarge your project, you will have to deal with a large number of partners, and during the discussions, it will be appreciated to be able to show your general culture. This is a good sign.

If you are an undergraduate student, you may want to know which study field to major and minor in. Reading is extremely important, really.

As the famous French writer Antoine Albalat said:

"To learn is to grow; to learn is to enlarge one's life."

Antoine Albalat

We don't say it enough, but learning is essential to reach success. Even famous entrepreneurs practice this activity on a daily basis.

Note that "success" is a very wide notion. Each of us has a different definition of what success may represent. One's success can be to be the richest man in the cemetery, while another person's success may be the fact that his / her children study well, and seize the opportunities that weren't given to him / her. Never compare yourself to other people. Your biggest enemy is yourself.

4. They focus on success: perseverance

Running a business is a liberal job that requires a very solid mind. An entrepreneur's day is made up of ups and downs, doubts and failures. You may need to be prone to a large number of falls and losses before getting a positive result.

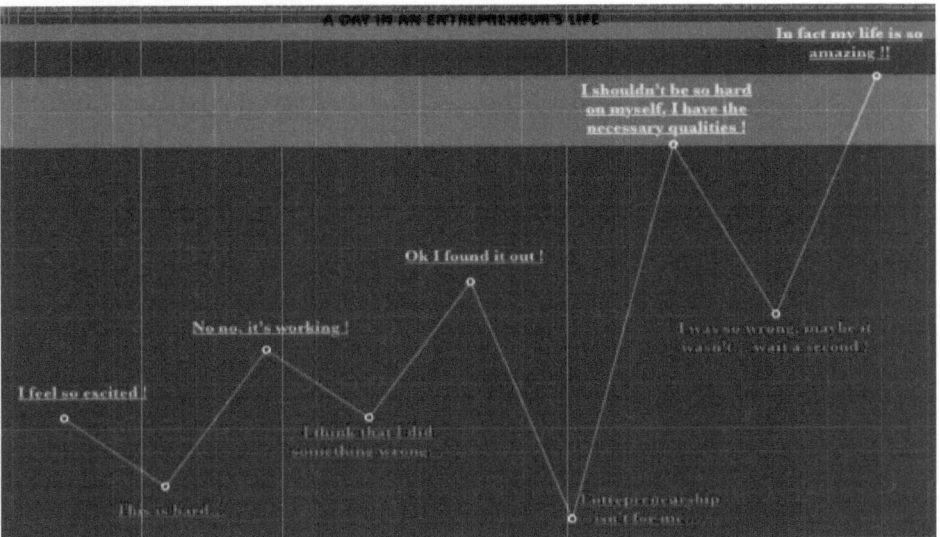

It was the case of Thomas Edison who had to file a thousand patents before creating the incandescent lamp (in 1879) that we use even today. Every entrepreneur, from the best known to the least known, had to fail several times before reaching the top.

Denzel Washington will certainly agree with this point when he said that:

"Ease is the greatest threat to progress, much more than adversity"

<u>Denzel Washington</u>

It is important not to give up during difficult times. On the contrary, you must be delighted to see the level of difficulty increase because it means that you are in progress, and that is exactly what you are looking for!

As the British President Winston Churchill said:

"It's when the night is deep that stars shine."

<u>Winston Churchill</u>

Failures will be the best moments in your journey as you learn new skills, and these will push you appreciate even more the moments of glory. Enjoy them, and stay focused on your primary goals.

5. They dream big

Human beings' dream faculty is unique to them, and it can help them achieve success. Of course, we are not talking about the dreams that you do when sleeping, but rather the goals that seem impossible to achieve. We are currently living the period during which it is too easy to earn money, at the point that some people become too lazy to even read a single book!

You can launch your e-commerce store from now on with single clicks. No more than 50$ are needed to do so, isn't it amazing? Previously, people who wanted to establish their own company had to assemble a large number of documents, raise an enormous fund of money, with the risk of losing everything at once. Nowadays, social medias made it so easy to make money online!

Keep in mind that before the creation of light bulbs by Joseph Swan (1878) and their improvement by Thomas Edison (1879), the only light source that was used since the human era was the candle. Before 1878, the only light source was logically that which emanated from the candles and nothing new could logically do it.

It is precisely this "logic" mindset that must be abolished. When you think with "logic", you no longer dream. And without dreams, we cannot innovate anything. Charlie Chaplin once said:

"We must strive for the impossible: the great exploits throughout history have been the conquest of what seemed impossible."

Charlie Chaplin

Being content with what already exists will not help you progress. You really need to aim for better, to set ever higher goals, to innovate ... To have a dream.

"Dreams are great. In fact, dreams are necessary in life,

otherwise no one would ever go anywhere! But a dream without aim and without action has no chance of being realized"

<u>Denzel Washington</u>

But setting goals without an action plan doesn't make sense. This is why you need to have a well-detailed <u>written</u> plan that puts bad habits aside. But also, you need to be in constant learning, and persistent. Everything is correlated, and success will only be within reach once you have followed these steps.

This is why you always need to keep a journal next to you.

6. They keep a journal to track their progress

Now that you have followed all these steps that we have detailed previously, it may happen to be doubtful concerning the path that you are following. Let me explain.

We previously talked about the "day of an entrepreneur", represented on a graph. It is steeped in ups and downs, joy and sadness, success and failure. This is why you always need to keep track of your progress. In fact, there are two main benefits that flow from this initiative.

First, you will know what you did great, and what you didn't. This way, you will quit bad habits and everything that keeps you away from reaching your goal. For instance, if you feel that you always need 30 minutes a day to reach all your daily goals, then you should wake up 30 minutes earlier. Also, if you believe that working with person A won't get you to the level you are aiming to get to, then you may look for someone else. Keep that person A as a friend maybe, but work with another one. Again, if person B isn't serious, answers too late, doesn't have the necessary skills, or is dishonest, you want to look for someone else. Always keep in mind that it is YOUR life, and that no one will get you closer to your goals if it's not you. You aren't responsible of others' behavior and failure, but you are responsible of yours. This is the reason why you need to take action as soon as possible!

Second, by keeping track of your progress, you will notice how amazing this process is. The satisfaction that flows from comparing yourself to the person you were a month ago is just amazing! And this is the fuel to your progress! I repeat, you will often face difficulties, and sometimes you will do it alone. To overcome these, you will have to use the soft skills that you have been improving since the beginning of this "self-improvement process":

- ❖ Motivation.
- ❖ Persistence.
- ❖ Self-confidence.

This journal can take several shapes. Indeed, you may summarize all the progresses you have made on a daily basis, at the end of the week or at the end of a period that you have chosen. The most important is to create such a journal.

I recommend you to do it on a daily basis. This way, you will be able to define the next day's goals, and the things that have to be changed.

X. LAST WORD: TAKE ACTION NOW!

Now that you've read the integrality of this book, you need to do an assessment of where you're at in your life. Are you satisfied of yourself? I sincerely hope that you answer negatively to this question.

Why? Because once you feel satisfied of yourself, you stop looking for improvement. Why would you get out of your comfort zone, and have this unpleasant feeling inside yourself that tells you that something is wrong? Yet, if you find something new to improve, however small it may be, you will feel proud of yourself for doing this much effort. You will feel that your life has sense.

You really don't want to look for the "easy path". The purpose of this book is to stimulate this tiny energy that resides in you, and that will evolve only if it is tested. It is the failures that allow this energy to grow. However, the facilities hinder the growth of this precious light. Remember, Les Brown once said that:

"Do what is easy and your life will be hard. Do what is hard and your life will become easy"

<u>Les Brown</u>

It's some kind of duty that you will have to do a day or another. The more you run away from your debts towards life, the less you will be ready to face them the day when the compound interest on these debts will be colossal.

I believe that you have all the tools you need to move forward. Really. Now it's up for you to use them in their entirety to become a new person: the one you dream of being for a long time!

If you need to, don't hesitate to read this book as many times as you need.

Good luck.

Balbacha El Mehdi.

FIRST EDITION

www.ingramcontent.com/pod-product-compliance
Lightning Source LLC
Chambersburg PA
CBHW030546220526
45463CB00007B/2997